MAY 9, 2010

A Special Gift

Karin
for

Grandma Fred
from

Happy Happy Mother's Day !

· *a family keepsake* ·

A
Mother's
LEGACY

your life story
in *your* own words

THOMAS NELSON
Since 1798

NASHVILLE   DALLAS   MEXICO CITY   RIO DE JANEIRO

Contents

Introduction

Days pass...seasons change... months meld into years, and we stand looking back at our lives—childhood memories, exciting moments, crises, and turning points.

In January we think of new beginnings; in February, of Valentine's Day, first dates, and first kisses. Does ever a June pass without thoughts of our own wedding day? Surely summer evokes backseat memories of seemingly unending trips to grandma's house or the beach. And don't November and December bring to mind family traditions and celebrations held tightly through the years?

Like ivy on the garden trellis, our lives are inescapably entwined with the seasons and months of the year. That is why we have designed this mother's memory journal in a twelve-month format. Each month features twelve intriguing questions with space to write a personal answer. Questions explore family history, childhood memories, lighthearted incidents, cherished traditions, and the dreams and spiritual adventures encountered in a lifetime of living.

Whether you choose to complete the journal in a few days, a few weeks, or over the course of a year, the questions will take you on a journey through the times and seasons of your life. This makes a tangible family record to pass on as a gift to a son or daughter. It's a loving memoir of written words that are windows for looking into a mother's heart.

No matter what your age, memory and reminiscence open a richer, fuller understanding of who you are as a family. Let this memory journal be a starting point—a door into discussing and sharing the unique qualities of your life. May *A Mother's Legacy* draw you closer to each other as you share the experiences of a lifetime.

PORTRAIT

YOUR FULL GIVEN NAME ....

YOUR DATE OF BIRTH ....

YOUR PLACE OF BIRTH ....

YOUR MOTHER'S FULL NAME ....

    the place and date of her birth..

    ....

YOUR FATHER'S FULL NAME ....

    the place and date of his birth..

    ....

THE NAMES OF YOUR PATERNAL GRANDPARENTS ....

    the places and dates of their births..

    ....

THE NAMES OF YOUR MATERNAL GRANDPARENTS ....

    the places and dates of their births..

    ....

THE NAMES OF YOUR SIBLINGS ....

    the places and dates of their births..

    ....

THE DATE AND PLACE OF YOUR MARRIAGE ....

THE FULL GIVEN NAME OF YOUR HUSBAND ....

THE NAMES AND BIRTHDATES OF YOUR CHILDREN ....

    ....

    ....

    ....

What Is Your Favorite?

FLOWER ....

PERFUME ....

COLOR ....

SONG ....

BOOK ....

AUTHOR ....

SAYING OR ....
QUOTATION
....

....

....

....

DESSERT ....

VACATION SPOT ....

TYPE OF FOOD ....

SPORT ....

MOVIE ....

LEISURE ACTIVITY ....

....

....

....

9

January

The beauty of the written word

is that it can be held

close to the heart

and read over and over again.

FLORENCE LITTAUER

WHAT WAS YOUR FAVORITE
PASTIME AS A CHILD?

*Did you prefer doing it alone
or with someone else?*

....
....
....
....
....
....
....
....
....
....
....
....
....
....
....
....
....
....
....
....
....

WHO GAVE YOU YOUR NAME
AND WHY?

....

....

....

....

....

....

....

....

....

Did you have
a family   ....
nickname?
How did you   ....
get it?
....

....

....

....

....

....

....

DESCRIBE YOUR
CHILDHOOD BEDROOM.

....

....

....

....

....

....

....

....

....

....

....

....

.... *What was*

.... *the view*

.... *from your*

.... *window?*

....

....

....

....

....

....

....

What was the silliest thing you ever did?

HOW OLD WERE YOU?

....
....
....
....
....
....
....
....
....
....
....
....
....
....
....
....
....
....
....
....
....
....
....

What were Saturdays like as a child?

Did you play sports?..
....
....
....

Visit grandparents?..
....
....
....

Was there a family dinner?..
....
....
....

If so, what was the typical menu?
....
....
....
....
....

WHERE DID YOUR FATHER
GO TO WORK EVERY DAY?

What did he do?

....
....
....
....
....
....
....
....
....
....
....
....
....
....
....
....
....
....
....
....
....

HOW DID YOUR MOTHER SPEND HER DAY?

Did she have a job or do volunteer work outside the home?

....
....
....
....
....
....
....
....
....
....
....
....
....
....
....
....
....
....
....
....
....
....
....
....

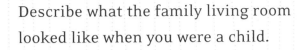

Describe what the family living room looked like when you were a child.

Did you have a favorite bedtime story that
you read before you went to sleep?
Who tucked you in?

....
....
....
....
....
....
....
....
....
....
....
....
....
....
....
....
....
....
....

Where was you childhood home? ....

....

....

Did you enjoy living there? ....

....

....

....

....

....

....

....

....

....

....

....

Describe your
grandparents' houses.

Did you visit them often?
Why or why not?

....
....
....
....
....
....
....
....
....
....
....
....
....
....
....
....
....
....
....
....
....

*List one special memory about
each of your brothers and sisters.*

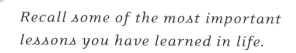

Recall some of the most important lessons you have learned in life.

....
....
....
....
....
....
....
....
....
....
....
....
....
....
....
....
....
....
....
....
....
....

February

For all of us,

today's experiences

are tomorrow's memories.

SHARE A MEMORY
OF YOUR GRANDPARENTS

or an older person you loved.

....
....
....
....
....
....
....
....
....
....
....
....
....
....
....
....
....
....
....
....
....
....
....
....
....
....

WHO HAVE YOU TURNED TO FOR ADVICE?

....
....
....
....
....
....
....
....
....
....
....
....
....
....
....
....
....
....
....
....
....
....
....
....
....
....

As a young girl, did you participate in sports, scouting, or some other organization or activity?

....
....
....
....
....
....
....
....
....
....
....
....
....
....
....
....
....
....
....
....
....

DO YOU REMEMBER A SPECIAL BOOK FROM YOUR CHILDHOOD?

Who gave it to you? Do you still have it?

....
....
....
....
....
....
....
....
....
....
....
....
....
....
....
....
....
....
....
....
....
....

DESCRIBE A MEMORABLE VALENTINE YOU RECEIVED.

....
....
....
....
....
....
....
....
....
....
....
....
....
....
....
....
....
....
....
....
....
....
....

How far did you have to travel to attend elementary, junior high, and high school, and how did you get there?

....
....
....
....
....
....
....
....
....
....
....
....
....
....
....
....
....
....
....
....
....
....
....

What scent or sound immediately takes you back to childhood?

....
....
....
....
....
....
....
....
....

Describe the feeling it evokes.

....
....
....
....
....
....
....
....
....
....
....
....
....

WHAT WAS YOUR FAVORITE MEAL WHEN YOU WERE A CHILD?

What made it your favorite?

What was the name of your favorite pet?

Why was it your favorite?

WHAT CHORES DID YOU HAVE TO DO WHEN YOU WERE GROWING UP?

Which ones did you dislike most?
Which did you not mind doing?

....
....
....
....
....
....
....
....
....
....

Did you get an allowance? How much was it?

....
....
....
....
....
....
....
....
....
....
....
....

Describe your first job.

....
....
....
....
....
....
....
....
....
....
....
....
....
....
....
....
....
....
....
....
....
....
....
....

SHARE YOUR FAVORITE
DESSERT RECIPE:

....
....
....
....
....
....
....
....
....
....
....
....
....
....
....
....
....
....
....
....
....
....
....
....
....
....

SHARE A "BAD WEATHER" STORY -
getting caught in a hailstorm,
living without power,
being housebound for days
during a big snowfall.

....
....
....
....
....
....
....
....
....
....
....
....
....
....
....
....
....
....
....
....
....
....
....
....
....
....

March

The mother's heart

is the child's schoolroom.

HENRY WARD BEECHER

CAN YOU RECALL AN ESPECIALLY INTERESTING VISITOR TO YOUR HOME?

What made that person or the occasion memorable?

WHAT DID YOU WANT TO BE
WHEN YOU GREW UP?

....
....
....
....
....
....
....
....
....
....
....
....
....
....
....
....
....
....
....
....
....
....
....
....
....
....

*What kinds
of things
do you do
to relax
or renew?
Do you have
a special
place you
like to go?*

WHO WAS YOUR FAVORITE TEACHER?
Why?

....
....
....
....
....
....
....
....
....
....
....
....
....
....
....
....
....
....
....
....
....
....
....
....

DESCRIBE ONE OF YOUR FAVORITE DRESS-UP OUTFITS AS A CHILD.

....
....
....
....
....
....
....
....
....
....
....
....
....
....
....
....
....
....
....
....
....
....
....
....
....
....

*Did you ever have a special
hideaway or playhouse?*

....
....
....
....
....
....
....
....
....
....
....
....

*What made
it special?*

....
....
....
....
....
....
....
....
....

WHAT EXTRACURRICULAR ACTIVITIES WERE YOU INVOLVED IN DURING HIGH SCHOOL?

Why did you choose those activities?

....
....
....
....
....
....
....
....
....
....
....
....
....
....
....
....
....
....
....

WHAT IS THE HARDEST THING
YOU EVER HAD TO DO?

....

....

....

....

....

....

....

What crazy fads do you remember in grade school?

....

....

....

....

....

....

....

....

....

....

....

....

....

....

....

....

....

When did you have your first date?

....
....
....
....
....
....
....
....
....
....
....
....
....
....
....
....
....
....
....
....
....
....
....
....

54

What do you remember about your first kiss?

....
....
....
....
....
....
....
....
....
....
....
....
....
....
....
....
....
....
....
....
....
....
....
....
....
....

What did you do to celebrate birthdays
when you were growing up?

....
....
....
....
....
....
....
....
....
....
....
....
....
....
....
....
....
....
....
....
....
....
....

Record here some gardening or decorating tips
that you have found helpful:

....
....
....
....
....
....
....
....
....
....
....
....
....
....
....
....
....
....
....
....
....
....
....
....
....

April

However time or circumstance
may come between a mother
and her child, their lives are
interwoven forever.

PAM BROWN

WHAT ARE SOME OF THE MOST MEMORABLE BOOKS YOU READ AS A CHILD?

....
....
....
....
....
....
....
....
....
....
....
....
....
....
....
....
....
....
....
....
....
....
....
....

What made them memorable?

What were your family finances like
when you were growing up?

....
....
....
....
....
....
....
....
....
....
....
....
....

How did that
affect you?

....
....
....
....
....
....
....
....
....
....

TELL ABOUT AN AWARD, HONOR, OR SPECIAL RECOGNITION YOU HAVE RECEIVED.

....
....
....
....
....
....
....
....
....
....
....
....
....
....
....
....
....
....
....

63

WHAT MISCHIEVOUS CHILDHOOD EXPERIENCE DO YOU REMEMBER?

How did it affect you?

....
....
....
....
....
....
....
....
....
....
....
....
....
....
....
....
....
....
....
....
....

What meaningful advice did you
receive from an adult?

What were the circumstances?

....
....
....
....
....
....
....
....
....
....
....
....
....
....
....
....
....
....
....
....
....
....
....

As a teenager did you rebel
or do things your parents
wouldn't have approved of?

....
....
....
....
....
....
....

How do
you feel
about
that now?

....
....
....
....
....
....
....
....
....
....
....
....
....
....
....

WHEN DID YOU FIRST LEARN
ABOUT SEX?

....
....
....
....
....
....
....
....
....
....   *What*
....   *was your*
....   *reaction?*
....
....
....
....
....
....
....
....
....
....

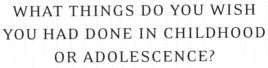

WHAT THINGS DO YOU WISH YOU HAD DONE IN CHILDHOOD OR ADOLESCENCE?

WHAT ARE THE THINGS
YOU ARE MOST GLAD YOU TRIED?

DESCRIBE YOUR MOTHER
IN HER BEST DRESS.

....
....
....
....
....
....
....
....
....
....
....
....
....
....
....
....
....
....
....
....
....
....

DESCRIBE YOUR FATHER
IN HIS WORKING CLOTHES.

What did your family like to do on weekends?

....
....
....
....
....
....
....
....
....

Describe one particularly memorable event.

....
....
....
....
....
....
....
....
....
....
....
....
....
....
....
....
....

Share one of your mother's best recipes

or a recipe for one of your favorite dishes.

....
....
....
....
....
....
....
....
....
....
....
....
....
....
....
....
....
....
....
....

May

In search of my mother's garden,

I found my own.

ALICE WALKER

WHAT TOYS DID YOU LIKE TO PLAY WITH?

Why those particular toys?

....
....
....
....
....
....
....
....
....
....
....
....
....
....
....
....
....
....
....
....
....
....

Describe a family trip and
why it was memorable.

WHAT IS ONE OF THE
MOST DIFFICULT CHOICES

you ever had to make?

....

....

....

....

....

....

*Would you
make the same
choice again?*

....

....

....

....

....

....

....

....

....

....

....

....

....

DO YOU REMEMBER A TIME WHEY YOU FELT OUT OF PLACE AND NOT WELCOME?

What did you do?

....
....
....
....
....
....
....
....
....
....
....
....
....
....
....
....
....
....
....

DID YOU EVER GO TO A DANCE?

What kind of car did your family drive?
Were you proud of it or embarrassed by it?
Why?

....
....
....
....
....
....
....
....
....
....
....
....
....
....
....
....
....
....

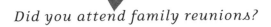

Did you attend family reunions?

....
....
....
....

Share a   ....
memory   ....
of one.   ....
                 ....

....
....
....
....
....
....
....
....
....
....
....
....
....
....
....
....

Did you go to gather with neighbors or friends?

....
....
....
....
....
....   *How*
....   *were they*
....   *important*
....   *to you and*
....   *your family?*
....
....
....
....
....
....
....
....
....
....
....
....
....
....
....

Tell about someone
   who influenced your life profoundly.

Tell me about your best childhood friend.

Where did you meet?

....
....
....
....
....
....

What secrets did you share?

....
....
....
....
....
....

What did you like to do?

....
....
....
....
....
....

IF YOU WENT TO COLLEGE
OR TO A CAREER TRAINING SCHOOL,

where did you go and why?

Where did you live when you were going to college or developing a career?

....
....
....
....
....
....
....
....

Describe an unforgettable experience from that time in your life.

....
....
....
....
....
....
....
....
....
....
....
....

What were your youthful goals and ambitions for your life?

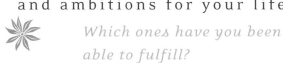

Which ones have you been able to fulfill?

....
....
....
....
....
....
....
....
....
....
....
....
....
....
....
....
....
....
....
....
....
....
....

ARE THERE CERTAIN WRITINGS THAT YOU REPEATEDLY TURN TO FOR ADVICE?

June

Women know

The way to rear up children (to be just)

They know a simple, merry, tender knack

Of tying sashes, fitting baby shoes,

And stringing pretty words that make no sense,

And kissing full sense into empty words.

ELIZABETH BARRETT BROWNING

IF YOU LEARNED TO PLAY A MUSICAL INSTRUMENT, TELL YOUR MEMORIES OF LESSONS, PRACTICE, AND YOUR MUSIC TEACHER.

If not, what instrument did you want to play and why?

What fashions were popular when you were in high school?

Did you like them? Why or why not?

....
....
....
....
....
....
....
....
....
....
....
....
....
....
....
....
....
....
....
....

WHAT DID YOU WEAR ON YOUR FIRST DATE WITH YOUR HUSBAND?

....
....
....
....
....
....
....
....
....
....
....
....
....
....
....
....
....
....
....
....
....
....
....

How old were you when you met your husband, and what attracted you to him?

....

....

....

....

....

....

....

....

....

....

....

....

....

....

....

....

....

....

....

....

....

....

....

WHEN DID YOU FIRST KNOW YOU WANTED TO MARRY HIM?

....
....
....
....
....
....
....
....
....
....
....
....
....

What made you feel that way?

....
....
....
....
....
....
....
....

.... *Share a*
.... *memory*
.... *about the*
.... *way he*
.... *proposed*
.... *to you.*
....
....
....
....
....
....
....
....
....
....
....
....
....
....
....
....
....

WHAT DID YOU WEAR
ON YOUR WEDDING DAY?

....
....
....
....
....
....
....
....
....
....
....
....
....
....
....
....
....
....
....
....
....
....

*Tell about your wedding day,
from beginning to end.*

....
....
....
....
....
....
....
....
....
....
....
....
....
....
....
....
....
....
....
....
....
....

Did your wedding ceremony include a special vow to each other?

....
....
....
....
....
....
....
....
....
....
....
....

What was the significance of it?..............................

....
....
....
....
....
....
....
....
....

Where did you go on your honeymoon?

Share one humorous incident.

....

....

....

....

....

....

....

....

....

....

....

....

....

....

....

....

....

....

WHAT WAS YOUR FIRST HOUSE
OR APARTMENT TOGETHER LIKE?

DO YOU REMEMBER ONE OF THE MEALS YOU FIXED AFTER YOU WERE MARRIED?

How has your cooking changed since then?

....
....
....
....
....
....
....
....
....
....
....
....
....
....
....
....
....
....
....
....
....
....

What do you love best about Dad now?

RECORD HERE SOME
TRAVEL TIPS OR SUGGESTIONS
FOR A FUN-FILLED VACATION:

July

I look back and see how I've

become who I am by a family

that found sweetness and joy

somewhere inside when . . . .

life experience tasted bitter.

KATHY BOICE

SHARE A FAMILY TRADITION OR MEMORY FROM THE FOURTH OF JULY.

....

....

....

....

....

....

....

....

....

....

....

....

....

....

....

....

....

....

....

....

....

....

....

....

What food and beverages were
served and who came to celebrate
with you?

....
....
....
....
....
....
....
....
....
....
....
....
....
....
....
....
....
....
....
....
....
....
....

Have you ever participated in a rally
or demonstration?

....
....
....
....
....
....
....
....
....
....
....

What was   ....
the cause?   ....
Why did you   ....
participate?   ....

....
....
....
....
....
....

Who in your family served in the military and when?
Do you have a special memory of that person?

....
....
....
....
....
....
....
....
....
....
....
....
....
....
....
....
....
....
....
....

DID YOU LEARN TO SWIM? HOW?

Did your family take vacations?
Record one especially memorable
experience.

....
....
....
....
....
....
....
....
....
....
....
....
....
....
....
....
....
....
....
....
....

Tell about your first trip by plane, train or ship.

....

....

....

....

....

....

How old were you? ....

....

....

Were you excited? Nervous? ....

....

....

....

....

....

....

....

....

....

....

....

IF YOU EVER TRAVELED ABROAD, WHAT WAS THE MOST UNIQUE PLACE YOU WENT?

If you haven't been abroad, what foreign country would you most like to visit? Why?

....
....
....
....
....
....
....
....
....
....
....
....
....
....
....
....
....
....
....

115

Describe the most fascinating place you have visited.

....
....
....
....
....
....
....
....
....
....
....
....
....
....
....
....
....
....
....
....
....
....
....

TELL ABOUT A DRIVING TRIP WITH YOUR FAMILY.

....
....
....
....
....
....
....
....
....
....
....
....
....
....
....
....
....
....
....
....
....
....
....

DID YOUR RELATIVES COME TO VISIT IN THE SUMMER OR DID YOU GO TO VISIT THEM?

....

....

....

....

....

....

....

....

....

....

....

....

....

What ....

are your ....

memories ....

of those ....

visits? ....

....

....

....

....

....

....

HOW DID YOU LEARN TO DRIVE?

What was your first car like?

....
....
....
....
....
....
....
....
....
....
....
....
....
....
....
....
....
....
....
....
....
....
....

DID A TRAGEDY EVER STRIKE
YOUR FAMILY?

....
....
....
....
....

How
were you   ....
affected?   ....
                ....
....
....
....
....
....
....
....
....
....
....
....
....
....
....

....

....

....

....

....

....

....

....

....

....

....

....

....

....

....

....

....

....

....

....

....

....

....

....

Share a favorite poem or a passage of writing that has been especially meaningful in your life.

August

The family–

that dear octopus from whose tentacles

we never quite escape,

nor, in our inmost hearts, ever quite wish to.

DODIE SMITH

NAME A BOOK OR AUTHOR THAT HELPED YOU DEVELOP A PHILOSOPHY OF LIFE.

*Share some
of these
insights.*

124

DID YOU HAVE A COLLECTION WHEN YOU WERE GROWING UP?

What initially sparked your interest in it?

DESCRIBE A PERFECT
SUMMER DAY.

....
....
....
....
....
....
....
....
....
....
....
....
....
....
....
....
....
....
....
....
....

What kind of outdoor work do
you like? Hate? Why?

If you could be a patron of a charity or organization, which one would you choose? Why?

....
....
....
....
....
....
....
....
....
....
....
....
....
....
....
....
....
....
....
....
....
....
....
....

WHEN DID YOU LEARN HOW TO RIDE A BIKE,

or to water ski, snow ski, rollerskate, or sail?

....
....
....
....
....
....
....
....

Share your memories of the experiences.

....
....
....
....
....
....
....
....
....
....
....

What summer activities did your family enjoy?

....
....
....
....
....
....
....
....
....
....
....
....
....
....
....
....
....
....
....
....

DID YOU EVER MILK A COW OR SPEND TIME ON A FARM OR IN THE COUNTRY?

....
....
....
....
....
....
....
....
....
....
....
....
....
....
....
....
....
....
....
....
....
....
....
....
....

Describe your first trip taken alone.

....
....
....
....
....
....
....
....
....
....
....
....
....
....
....
....
....
....
....
....
....
....
....

WHAT PLACES WOULD YOU STILL LIKE TO VISIT?
Why?

....
....
....
....
....
....
....
....
....
....
....
....
....
....
....
....
....
....
....
....
....
....
....

DESCRIBE A FRIGHTENING OR DIFFICULT EXPERIENCE FROM CHILDHOOD. HOW DID YOU RESPOND TO IT?

Tell me about your most unforgettable summer experience as a child.

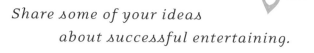

Share some of your ideas
  about successful entertaining.

....
....
....
....
....
....
....
....
....
....
....
....
....
....
....
....
....
....
....
....
....
....
....
....
....

September

Our lives are a mosaic of little things,

like putting a rose

in a vase on the table.

INGRID TROBISCH

DID YOU LEARN TO SEW OR MAKE OTHER CRAFTS?

How and when?

....
....
....
....
....
....
....
....
....
....
....
....
....
....
....
....
....
....
....
....
....
....
....

What was the first thing you made?

....

....

....

....

....

....

....

....

....

....

....

....

....

....

....

....

....

....

....

TELL ABOUT A SPECIAL OUTING YOU TOOK WITH YOUR MOTHER OR YOUR FATHER.

....
....
....
....
....
....
....
....
....
....
....
....
....
....
....
....
....
....
....
....
....
....

*What was the most
tender day in your childhood?*

....
....
....
....
....
....
....
....
....
....
....
....
....
....
....
....
....
....
....
....
....
....

WHAT WERE YOUR FAVORITE
SUBJECTS IN GRADE SCHOOL?

....

....

....

....

junior high? ....

....

....

....

....

high school? ....

....

....

....

What was your major in college? ....

....

....

Would you choose that major again?
Why or why not? ....

....

....

....

....

....

....

144

As a young person, did you volunteer for work in your community?

....

....

....

....

....

....

....

....

....

Tell me ....

about your ....

experiences. ....

....

....

....

....

....

....

....

....

....

....

....

....

When did you move away from home?

....
....
....
....
....
....

Describe where you lived and how you felt about it.

....
....
....
....
....
....
....
....
....
....
....
....
....
....
....

WHO WAS YOUR BEST FRIEND
AFTER YOU WERE MARRIED?

*Describe some of the fun things you
did together. Are you still friends?*

WHAT ARE YOUR STRENGTHS?

....
....
....
....
....
....
....
....
....
....
....
....
....
....
....
....
....
....
....

What is something you learned from an especially happy time in your life?

....
....
....
....
....
....
....
....
....
....
....
....
....
....
....
....
....
....
....
....
....
....

WHAT SPECIAL TALENTS DID YOUR PARENTS NURTURE IN YOU?

....
....
....
....
....
....
....
....
....
....

How have you
developed
those talents?

....
....
....
....
....
....
....
....
....
....

What would you like to learn to do? Why?

....

....

....

....

....

....

....

....

....

....

....

....

....

....

....

....

....

....

....

....

....

....

....

WHAT WOULD YOU DO DIFFERENTLY IN LIFE IF YOU COULD?

....
....
....
....
....
....
....
....
....
....
....
....
....
....
....
....
....
....
....
....
....

October

How will our children
know who they are if
they don't know where
they came from?

MA, IN *THE GRAPES OF WRATH*

Who are some of the best speakers you have ever heard? Why?

HOW WOULD YOU LIKE TO BE REMEMBERED?

....

....

....

....

....

....

....

....

....

....

....

....

....

....

....

....

....

....

....

....

....

What are some of the things
that make you smile
when you think of them?

....
....
....
....
....
....
....
....
....
....
....
....
....
....
....
....
....
....
....
....
....
....
....

WHAT RESPONSIBILITIES
DID YOUR PARENTS REQUIRE
OF YOU AS A CHILD?

....
....
....
....
....
....
....

Explain   ....
how this   ....
affected your   ....
growth and   ....
development.   ....

....
....
....
....
....
....
....
....

NAME YOUR FAVORITE HOBBY.

When and where did you start doing it?
Why do you enjoy it?

....
....
....
....
....
....
....
....
....
....
....
....
....
....
....
....
....
....
....
....
....
....

WHEN AND WHERE DID YOU BUY YOUR FIRST HOUSE?

Describe the house and explain any significance it held for you.

....
....
....
....
....
....
....
....
....
....
....
....
....
....
....
....
....
....

WHAT IS THE STRANGEST THING YOU HAVE EVER SEEN?

....

....

....

....

....

....

....

....

....

....

....

....

....

....

....

....

....

....

....

....

....

....

TELL ABOUT A MEMORABLE HOTEL OR RESORT YOU HAVE VISITED.

Describe the location and tell about experiences that were significant.

....
....
....
....
....
....
....
....
....
....
....
....
....
....
....
....
....
....
....
....
....
....
....
....

DID YOU EVER GO ON A HAYRIDE
OR BOB FOR APPLES?

....
....
....
....
....
....
....
....
....

*What
other fun
activities
did you
and your
friends or
classmates
enjoy?*

....
....
....
....
....
....
....
....
....
....
....
....
....

AS A TEENAGER, DID YOU BELONG TO A CLUB OR ORGANIZATION?

Tell about the individuals in the group who were most significant to you.

....
....
....
....
....
....
....
....
....
....
....
....
....
....
....
....
....
....
....
....
....
....

SHARE SOME HELPFUL HOME REMEDIES OR TIPS FOR GOOD HEALTH.

November

In our family an experience was not finished,

nor truly experienced, unless written down

or shared with another.

ANNE MORROW LINDBERGH

WHAT INDIVIDUALS HAVE HAD THE GREATEST IMPACT ON YOUR LIFE?

....
....
....
....
....
....
....
....
....
....
....
....
....
....
....
....
....
....
....
....
....
....
....

In what way?

....
....
....
....
....
....
....
....
....
....
....
....
....
....
....
....
....
....
....
....
....

WHAT IS YOUR MOST TREASURED
POSSESSION AND WHY?

Who were your female role models
when you were growing up?

How have they affected the kind of person you are?

....
....
....
....
....
....
....
....
....
....
....
....
....
....
....
....
....
....
....
....
....
....
....
....

What is your most vivid memory of being pregnant?

....
....
....
....
....
....
....
....
....
....
....
....
....
....
....
....
....
....
....
....
....
....
....
....
....
....
....

HOW DID YOU CHOOSE
YOUR CHILDREN'S NAMES AND WHY?

....
....
....
....
....
....
....
....
....
....
....
....
....
....
....
....
....
....
....
....
....
....
....
....
....

WHAT IS YOUR MOST POIGNANT MEMORY
ABOUT YOUR CHILD'S LIFE?

What was a favorite
Thanksgiving tradition
in your family?

WHAT ARE SOME THINGS FROM YOUR CHILDHOOD THAT YOU ARE THANKFUL FOR?

What childhood memory first comes to mind when you think about winter?

How do you respond to that memory?

....
....
....
....
....
....
....
....
....
....
....
....
....
....
....
....
....
....
....
....

What are some of the things you remember most from your childhood experiences at school or in your neighborhood?

....
....
....
....
....
....
....
....
....
....

Do certain people come to mind?

....
....
....
....

....
....
....
....
....
....
....
....
....

WHAT FAMILY CUSTOM WOULD YOU LIKE TO PASS ON TO YOUR CHILDREN AND GRANDCHILDREN?

WHAT NEW TRADITION WOULD YOU LIKE TO START IN THE FAMILY?

What is its significance?

....
....
....
....
....
....
....
....
....
....
....
....
....
....
....
....
....
....
....
....
....
....
....
....

Share a favorite Thanksgiving or
Christmas recipe.

....
....
....
....
....
....
....
....
....
....
....
....
....
....
....
....
....
....
....
....
....
....
....
....
....

December

I will honor Christmas in my heart,

and try to keep it all the year.

CHARLES DICKENS

TELL ABOUT SOME CHRISTMAS RITUALS IN YOUR FAMILY

and how you felt about them.

WERE YOU EVER IN A CHRISTMAS PROGRAM? HOW DID YOU RESPOND TO THE EXPERIENCE?

What favorite Christmas treasures have you kept from year to year? Share their origins.

TELL ABOUT A MEMORABLE
CHRISTMAS WITH RELATIVES.

What is your favorite Christmas carol?

....
....
....
....
....

Why? ....
....
....
....
....
....
....
....
....
....
....
....
....
....
....
....
....

DID YOU HAVE A CHRISTMAS STOCKING OR A SPECIAL ORNAMENT AS A CHILD?

What did it look like?

Describe the Christmas that has been the most meaningful to you.

....
....
....
....
....
....
....
....
....
....
....
....
....
....
....
....
....
....
....
....
....
....
....
....
....
....

What would be the most wonderful gift you could receive? Why?

What have people older than you taught you about life? What have you learned from children and young people?

....
....
....
....
....
....
....
....
....
....
....
....
....
....
....
....
....
....
....
....
....
....

WHAT WOULD YOU LIKE TO SEE HAPPEN IN THE NEXT TEN YEARS?

WHAT WAS ONE OF THE BEST SURPRISES YOU EVER HAD?

A party? A gift? An unexpected favor?

....
....
....
....
....
....
....
....
....
....
....
....
....
....
....
....
....
....
....
....
....
....

*What word best describes
your life? Explain why.*

....
....
....
....
....
....
....
....
....
....
....
....
....
....
....
....
....
....
....
....
....
....
....
....
....

What advice about life do you want others to remember?

....
....
....
....
....
....
....
....
....
....
....
....
....
....
....
....
....
....
....
....
....
....
....

NOTES

NOTES

NOTES

NOTES

PHOTOS

PHOTOS

PHOTOS

PHOTOS

PHOTOS